D0116682

Camp Grandma®

Camp Grandma

Grandma's Favorite ♥ Memories

By Jessica H. Breedlove

All artwork ©2003 Jessica Breedlove

I
dedicate this book
to my "Geema",
Henrietta Law,
who brought magic into
my world as a child
and continues to inspire me
to this day.

Much love,
Your Jessie Bess

When a child is born,
so is a Grandmother...

~ Italian Proverb

Camp Grandma Dedication:

On this .... day of ....

I, ... dedicate this book of memories
(Grandma)

to ...., my dearest
(Grandchild's Name)

.... so that you may never forget
(Grand Son or Daughter)

the magic, laughter, story, and tradition

of family before you.

We find rest in those we love, and we provide a resting place in ourselves for those who love us.

—St. Bernard of Clairaux

Grandma's Parents

Grandchild, you would make my parents so happy and proud. I want you to remember this about them: ....

....

....

....

....

My mother's name : ....

It means : ....

She is originally from : ....

She was born on : ....

My favorite memory of my mother : ....

....

My father's name : ....

It means: ....

He is originally from: ....

He was born on: ....

My favorite memory of my father: ....

....

Grandma's Parents

My parents would want you always to remember:

....

....

....

....

....

....

....

....

....

....

....

....

....

....

....

It is as Grandmothers that our mothers come into the fullness of their Grace.
—Christopher Morley

Grandma's Parents

Favorite Photos

GRAND  PHOTOS

Gratitude looks to the Past and Love to the Present. ~C.S. Lewis

Mother..

Grandma ....

Grandpa..............................

Great Grandma..........................

Great Grandpa..........................

Great Grandpa..........................

Great Grandma..........................

When I, your GRANDMA was a baby......

I was born on .... in .... , ...
<small>(city)</small>   <small>(State)</small>

I weighed .... and was .... long

My parents named me : ....

I am named after : ....

It means : ....

....

....

They proudly showed me off and said I was the spitting image of :

....

....

My first home was : ....

....

....

....

GrandMa's Photos

baby

My parents' favorite memory of me as a baby was the time I :

....
....
....
....
....
....
....

It's a girl!

When I was growing up, many things were different than they are now. I didn't have today's complicated electronic toys to play with...

Instead, my favorite toys were :...
....
....
....

My favorite pets were :..
....

My favorite hiding places were :...
....

My favorite hobbies were :..
....
....
....

But even though the world was
different in this way...

....
....
....
....
....
....
....
....
....
....
....
....
....

Some things never change
no matter when you grew up...

My favorites

The taste of ice cream, the feel of a summer breeze on your face,
winning a race, climbing a tree, humming a tune, hugging your best
friend. As a child I had many favorites probably quite similar
to yours...

My favorite season : .... My favorite color : ....
....

My favorite friends : ....
....
....

My favorite foods : ....
....
....

My favorite places : ....
....
....

My favorite Rainy Day Past-times : ....
....
....

favorites

Camp Grandma

What I did in the Summer : ....
....
....

What I did in the Fall : ....
....
....

What I did in the Spring : ....
....
....

What I did in the Winter : ....
....
....

GRANDMA's favorite Childhood Memories

Grandma's Favorite
Childhood Photos

Grandma - 18 months

There is only one happiness in life, to Love and be Loved.
-George Sand

Your ☆ Grandpa

I met your Grandpa...
when I was................... years old. He was............................years old.

I will never forget how we met : ....

....

....

....

....

....

....

....

....

....

....

Your Grandpa and I have spent.................years together, and have been married for a total of................years.

My favorite thing about him at first was :

....

....

....

....

....

My favorite thing about him now is :

....

....

....

....

....

....

....

The first gift your Grandfather ever gave me was :

....

....

I will never forget the day your Grandfather asked me to marry him :

....

....

....

....

....

....

The First time I met Grandpa's Family :

....

....

....

....

Our Wedding Day

We were married on the .... day
of .... in the year ....
in ...., ...
     (City)   (State)

Our wedding day was unforgettable because :

....

....

....

....

....

....

....

I remember the weather was :

....

....

....

My wedding dress was made of..
and looked like :...

....

....

I wore my hair :..

....

My favorite memory of our wedding day :...

....

....

....

....

....

....

....

....

WEDDING ♥ PHOTOS

HONEYMOON

After our wedding we traveled to :

....

....

....

....

....

When we returned we began our married lives together.
My favorite memories of this time in our lives :

....

....

....

....

....

....

....

LOVE is always COOKIN' at

Growing Grandchild,

One of the sweetest gifts I can give you
are delicious treats to eat during
your visits to Camp Grandma.

Here are your favorites:

Camp Grandma

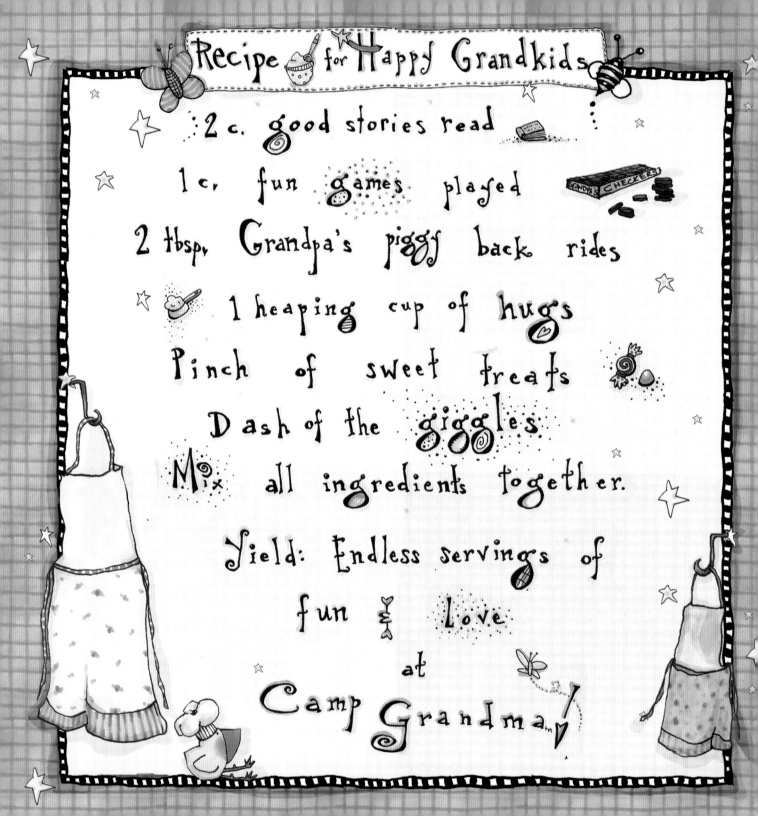

Recipe for Happy Grandkids

2 c. good stories read

1 c. fun games played

2 tbsp. Grandpa's piggy back rides

1 heaping cup of hugs

Pinch of sweet treats

Dash of the giggles

Mix all ingredients together.

Yield: Endless servings of
fun & Love
at
Camp Grandma!

Camp Grandma Cookin' School

I learned to cook when I was .... years old.
My .... taught me how.

My favorite memory of learning to cook is:

....

....

....

....

....

....

....

....

....

....

....

....   did some one say   ....
cookie?

My greatest cooking success was the time I :

....
....
....
....
....

My greatest cooking disaster was the time I tried to :

....
....
....
....
....
....
....

Famous for hugs & cookies

Cookies

there's No Place Like home...

except Camp Grandma

When you visit Camp Grandma,
your favorite things to eat are :

Favorite Breakfast :..

....

Favorite Lunch :...

....

Favorite Dinner :..

....

Favorite Snack :...

....

Favorite Dessert :..

....

Favorite kind of Cookie :..

....

My favorite things to eat
when you visit Camp Grandma are:

Favorite Breakfast :...

....

Favorite Lunch :..

....

Favorite Dinner :...

....

Favorite Snack :..

....

Favorite Dessert :..

....

Favorite kind of Cookie :...

....

favorite • Family • Recipes

for YOU to remember

Camp Grandma
is a very
special place
filled with
Grandma's love
and a much slower
pace.

There's always time
to bake
or fix a toy that's
broken —
Camp Grandma
is a special place
where "No" is rarely
spoken!

GRANDMA

i'll tell you a story,
and pour you some tea
i'll bake upside-down cake
that only we can see..

i'll mix and i'll stir,
i'll pour and i'll bake,
Mixing sugar and love
just to make you a cake.

there might be a few
of those things "they" call lumps
but you'll know cause i made them
- my love's in those bumps!

I love camp grandma

© 2003 Jessica Breedlove

Famous for tea and cookies

It's such a
Grand Thing
to be a Mother of a
Mother —
that's why the world
calls her a
GRaND
Mother!

—author unknown

Grandma

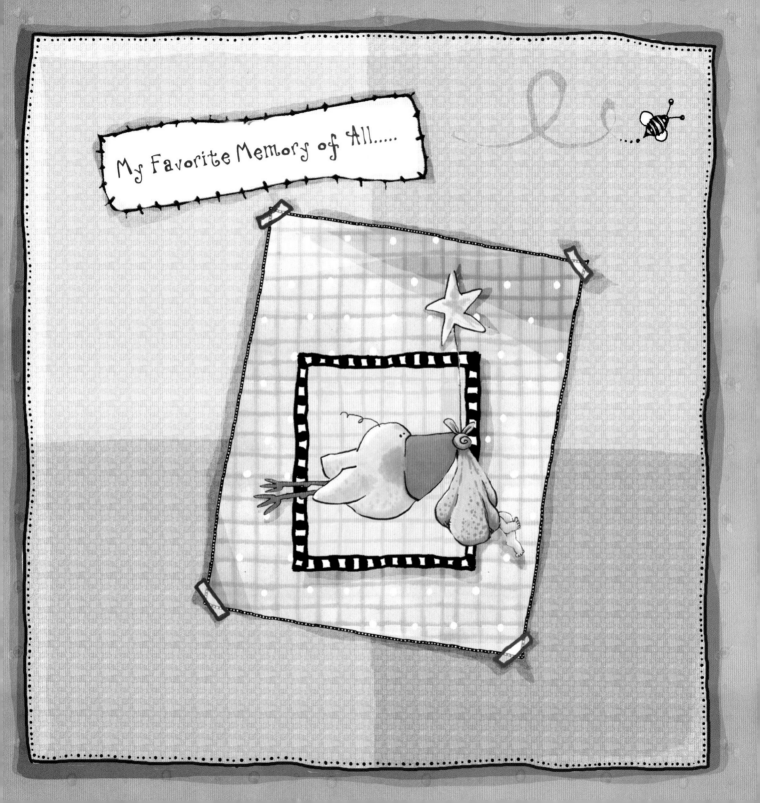

My Favorite Memory of All.....

is the Day you Arrived...

We came by car,

We came by train

By bike

and truck

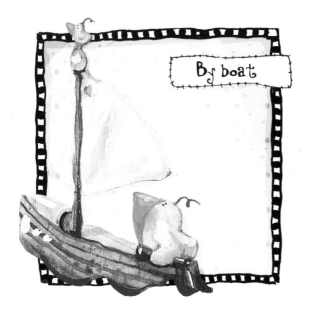

By boat

and plane

We came to see

our precious one

the
littlest star
our hearts had won.

Our GRANDbaby Arrives!

Our Precious Little Star :

....
(name)

Was Born :

the .... day of .... , ...
(Month)   (Year)

At .... o'clock

in

...., ...
(City)   (State)

Weighing :

.... lb. .... oz.

and

.... inches long

i'll never forget the first time i saw you :

....

....

....

....

....

....

....

....

....

....

....

....

i think you are the spitting image of : ....

....

....

....

....

....

All love is sweet,
Given or Returned...
-Percy Bysshe Shelly

GRANDbaby Photos

Soon you began to walk...

You were .... months old when you began to walk.
I'll never forget the first time you toddled toward me:

....

....

....

....

....

Not long after, you weren't just walking, but running and
we could barely keep up. I'll never forget:

....

....

....

....

....

...and talk

i LUV GWAMMA

The first time you spoke directly to me, you said :

....

....

....

....

....

Before you could pronounce my name, you called me :

....

....

The funniest things came out of your mouth.
I never want to forget when you said :

....

....

....

....

....

It was blustery cold
the wind whipping the air
frost on the windows
ice everywhere...

But inside Camp Grandma
we're snug little bugs
We tell stories, eat cookies,
wrapped up in a hug.

Sipping cocoa and tea
as the fire crackles away –
Grandma's love is so warm
on this cold blustery day.

Welcome to Camp Grandma

My favorite Winter Times spent with you, Dear Grandchild—
I will always remember :

....
....
....
....
....
....
....
....
....
....
....
....
....

My favorite Summer Memories spent with you are:

Grandpa

Activity Director

One of the BEST things about
Camp Grandma™ is Grandpa you see.
i love all the piggy back rides

And the games he plays with Me
He always makes sure

there's lots of FUN stuff to do.
My favorite place is Camp Grandma™....
'Cause Grandpa's there, too!

Welcome

Grandpa's *favorite* Memories

Favorite Activities you and Grandpa love to do together :

....
....
....
....
....
....
....
....
....
....

Grow

You've got to do your own Growing
No matter how tall your Grandfather was...

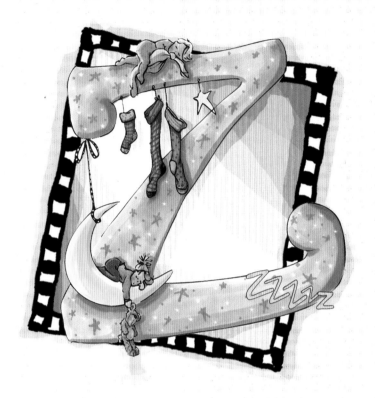